Hi, welcome to Festive fun this Christmas with 100 creative coloring pages!

Ideally suited for kids ages 1-4 as they discover the world around them. This book is intended to boost early childhood development through engaging activities that build connections with words, pictures and colors. All the custom artwork has been created by experienced designers to be the right level for kids to stimulate imagination, to allow them to build their fine motor skills and to have a load of fun and learning in the process!

With 100 big pages of illustrations, children will explore and enjoy a HUGE variety of easy to color Christmas designs.

Thank you for purchasing this book and we hope you and your little ones unlock a world of coloring fun and learning!
We're still learning and growing ourselves, so we'd really appreciate a review on Amazon for this book if you have time.
Thank you

Check out other titles in our TODDLER COLORING series!

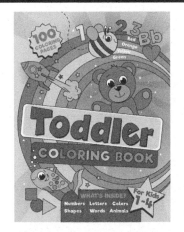

ISBN: 979-8552067565   ISBN: 979-8520557715

This

CHRISTMAS
Toddler
COLORING BOOK

BELONGS TO

....

MERRY CHRISTMAS!

WINTER IN THE WOODS

CHEEKY ELVES!

FUN IN THE SNOW

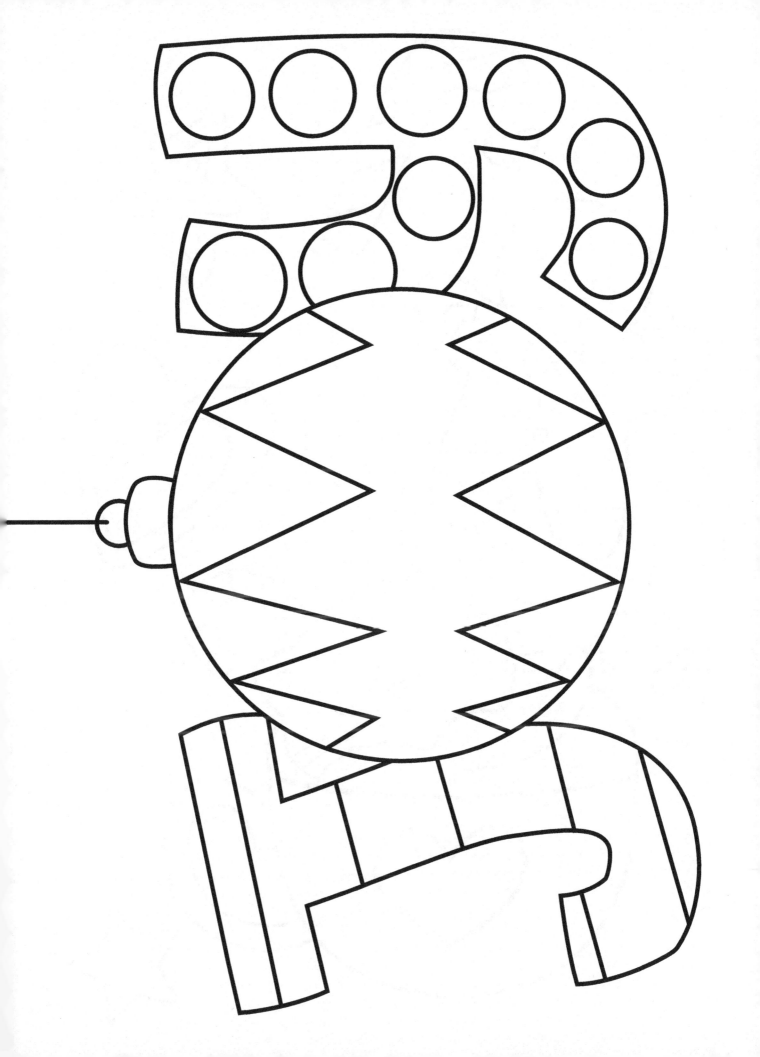

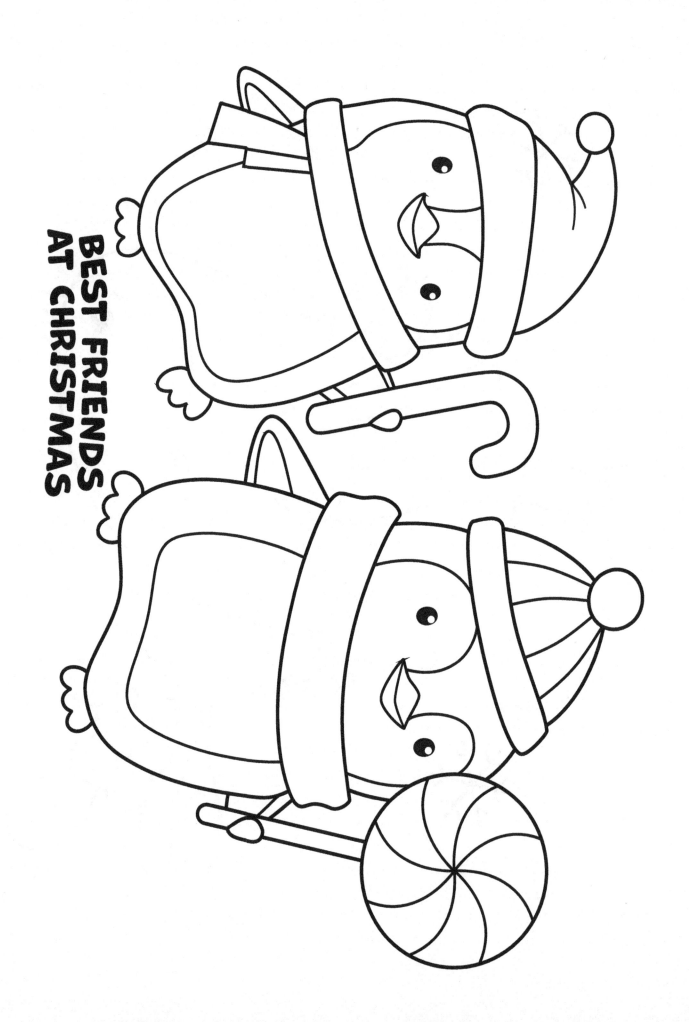

BEST FRIENDS
AT CHRISTMAS

SILLY

PENGUIN

Ready for
SNOW

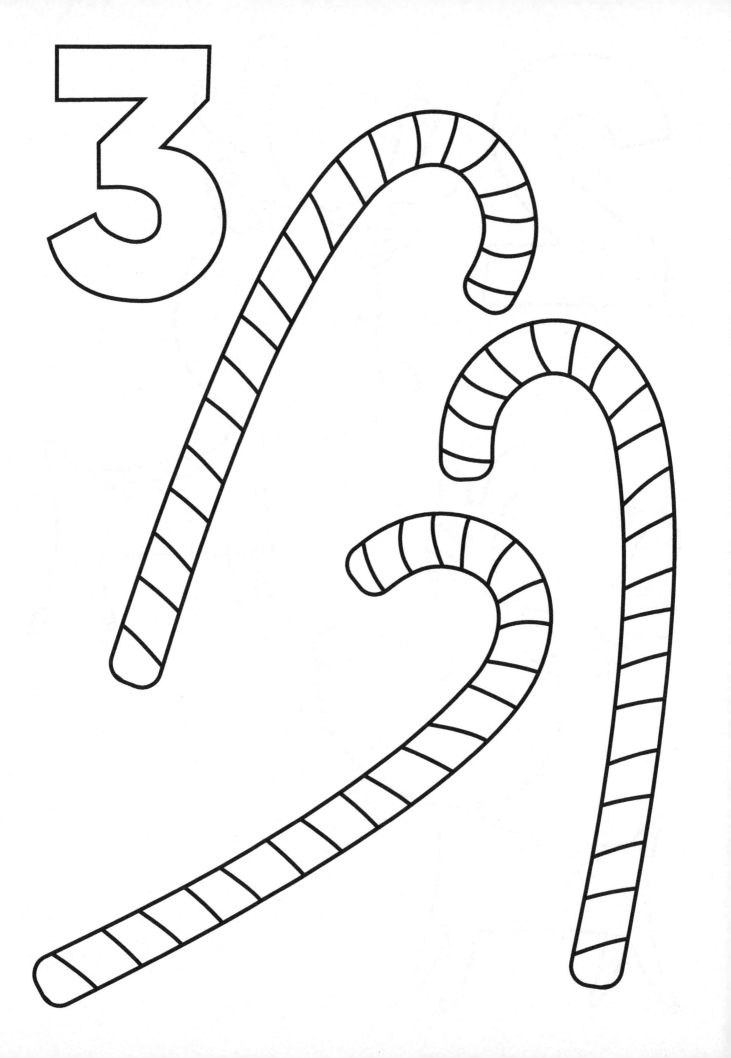

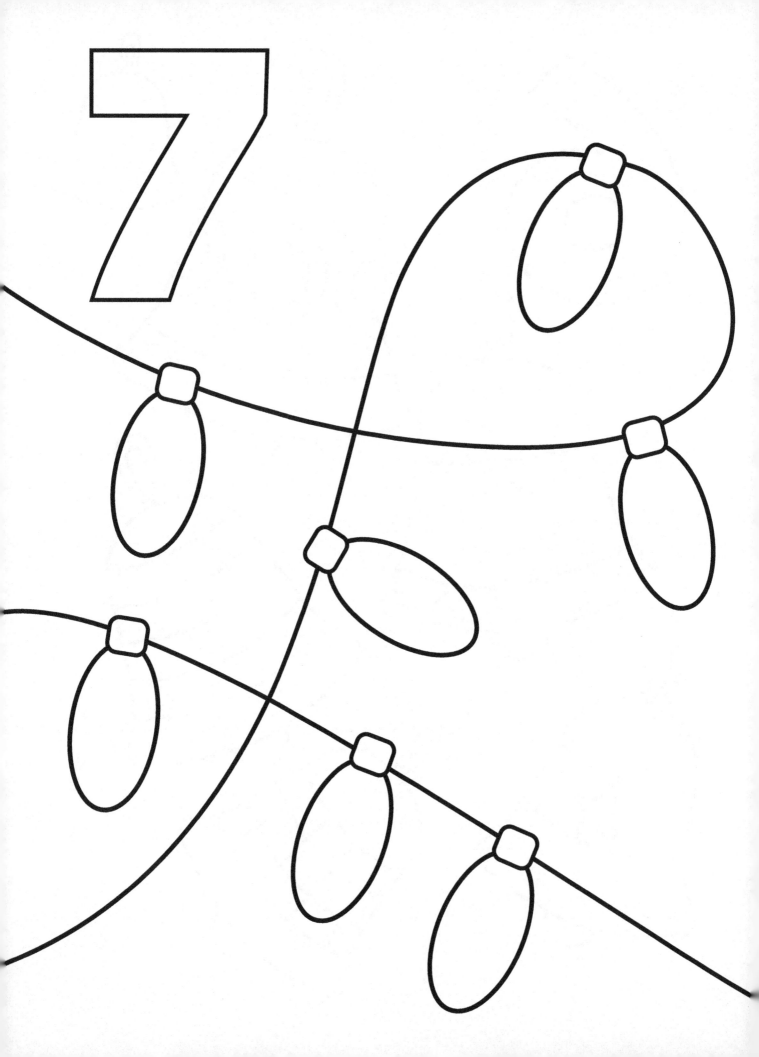

CHRISTMAS
TREATS

THE
NUTCRACKER

CHRISTMAS BEAR

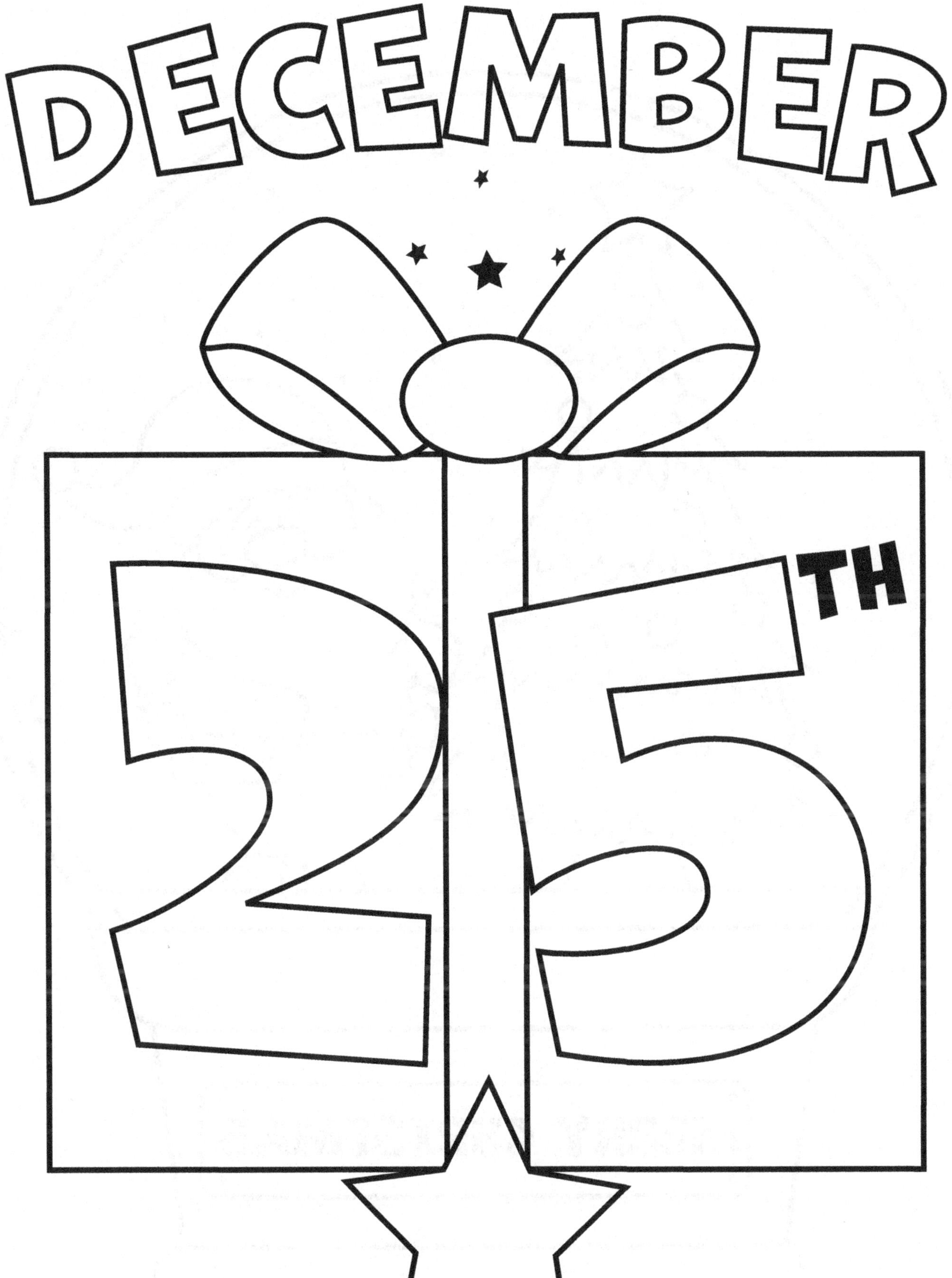
DECEMBER
25TH

Santa & Mrs
CLAUS

DRAW & COLOR YOUR OWN DECORATION ON BOTH SIDES OF THE PAPER. ASK A GROWN-UP TO CAREFULLY CUT IT OUT AND DISPLAY!

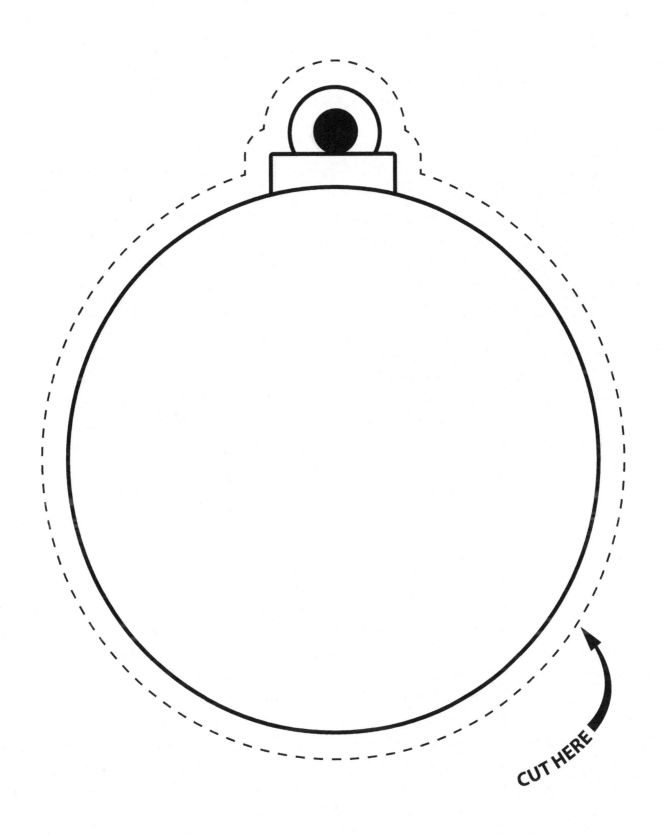

CUT HERE

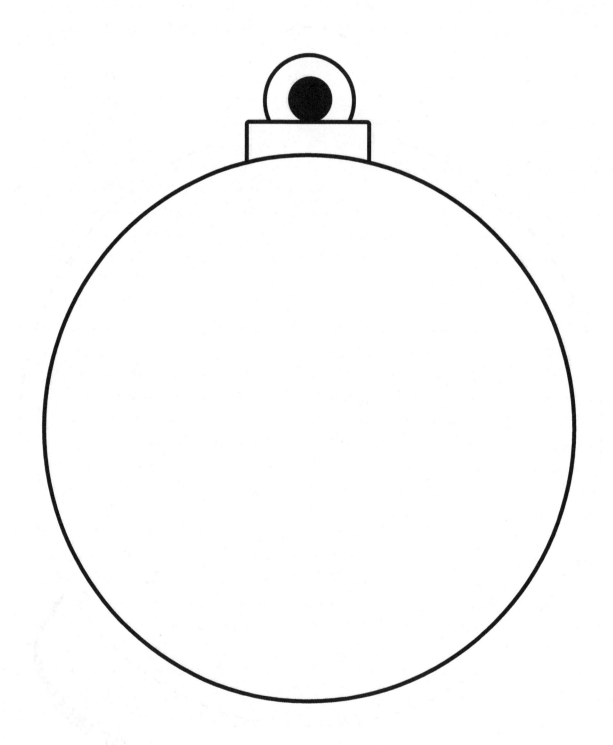

SPEEDY SANTA

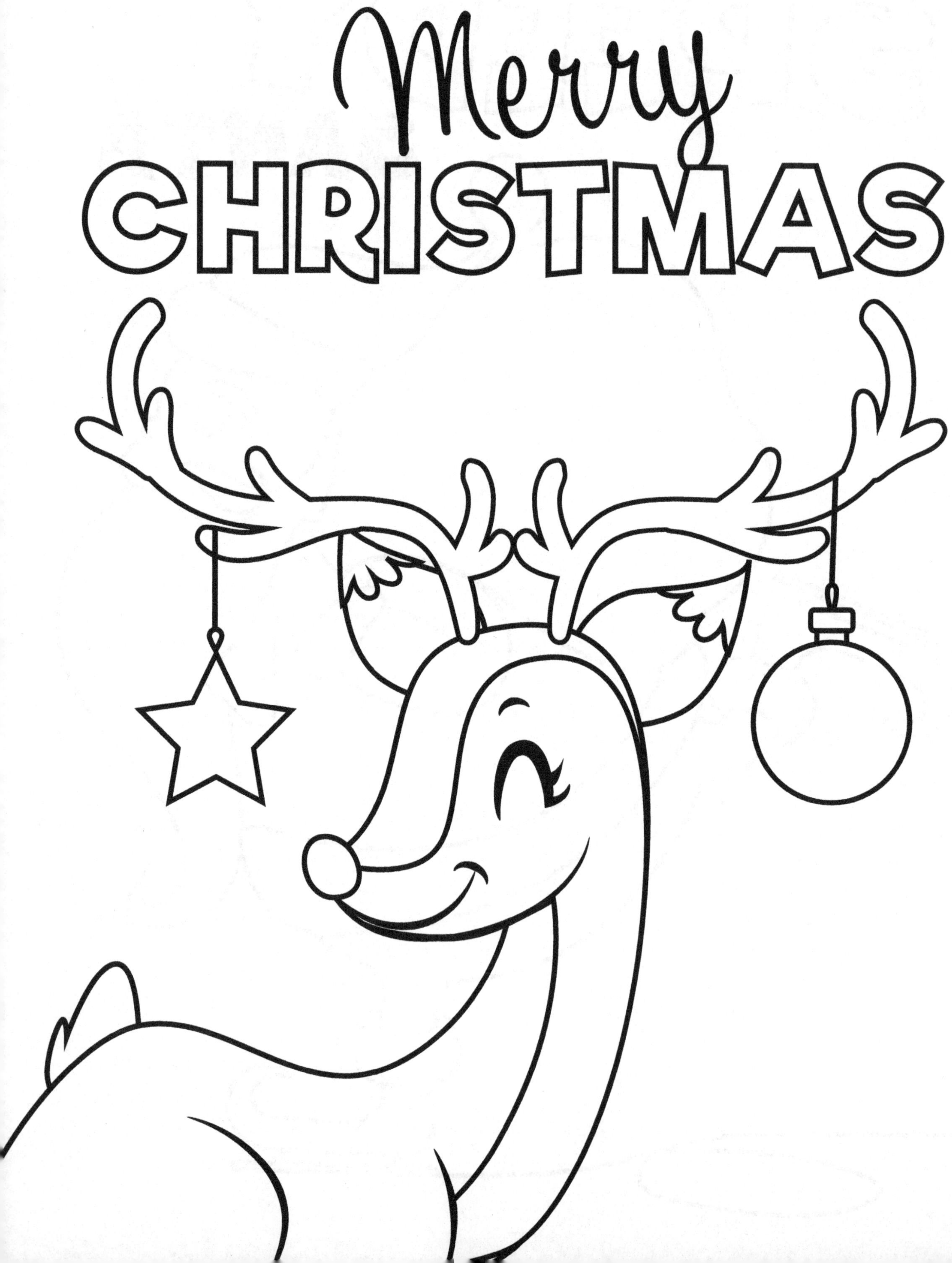
Merry
CHRISTMAS

TIME FOR GINGERBREAD

SNOWMAN

MERRY CHRISTMAS

TIME TO DRESS UP
COSY!

Dashing through the snow!

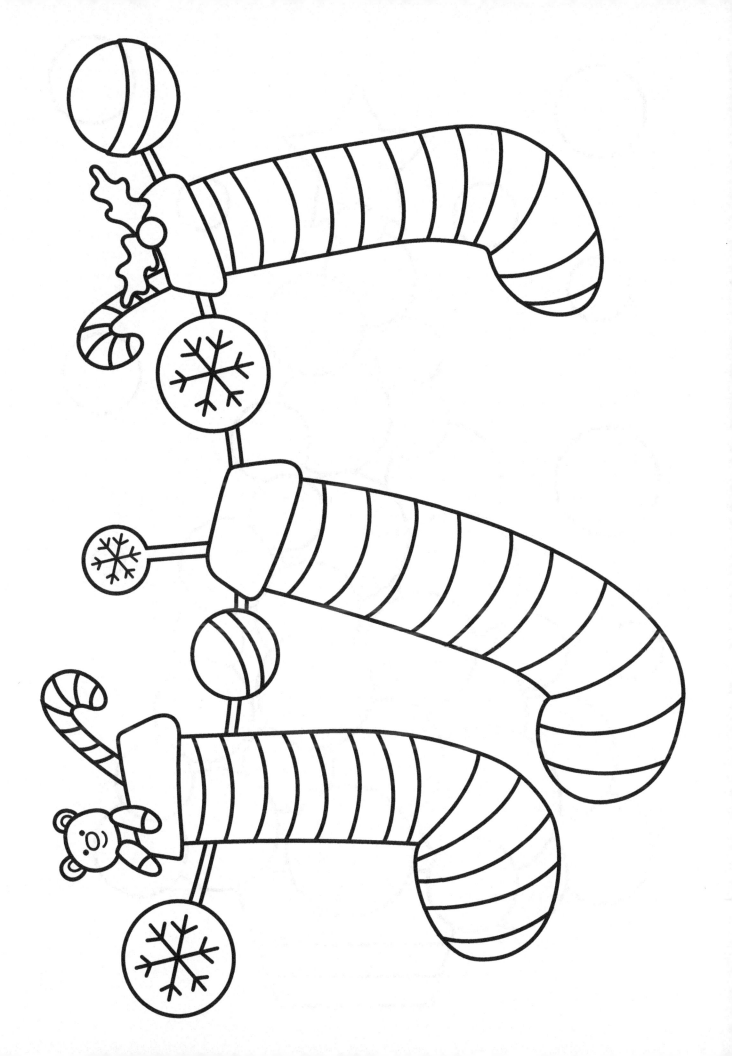

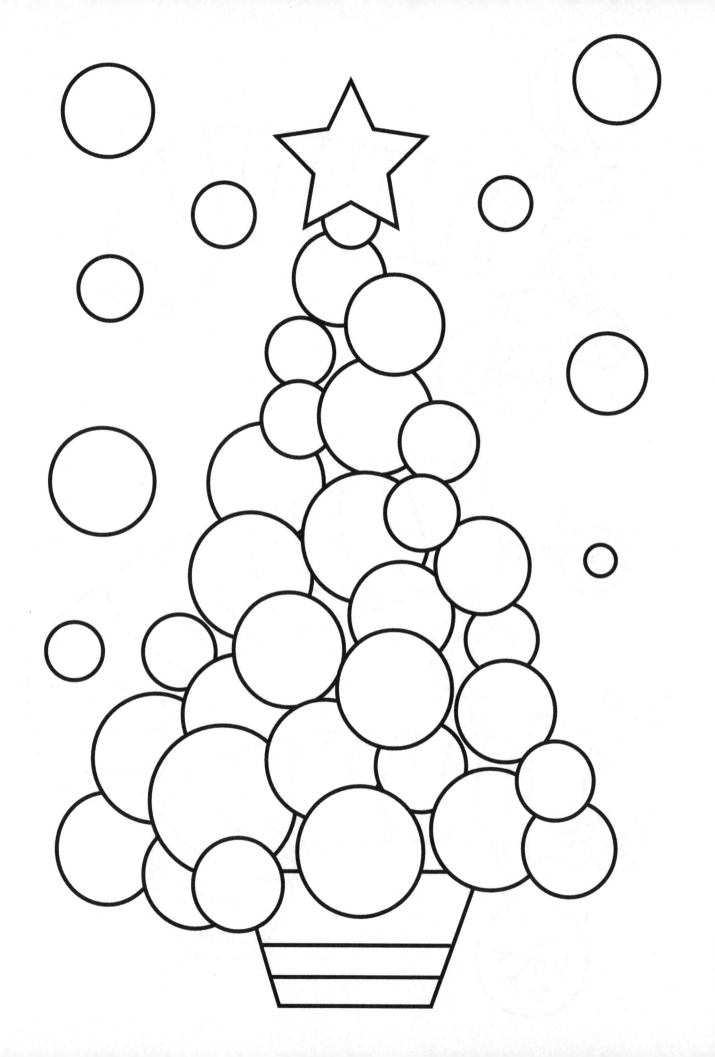

CHRISTMAS TREES!

CHRISTMAS SURPRISE !

Ready for Santa!

We hope you enjoyed this book. As we learn and grow, we'd love a rating or review for it on Amazon, if you have time. **Thank You!**

Loads more from Under The Cover Press available at amazon

ISBN 979-8864951200

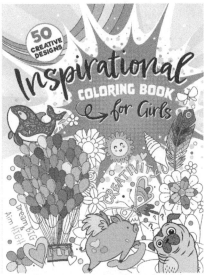

ISBN 979-8430304089

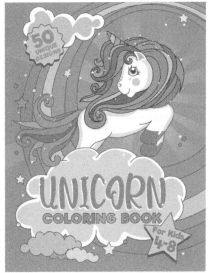

ISBN 979-8695161878

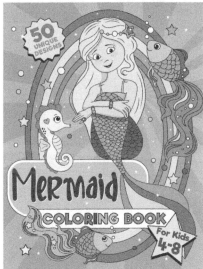

ISBN 979-8484253012

ISBN 979-8590346219

ISBN 979-8559845876

ISBN 979-8559850436

ISBN 979-8717778565

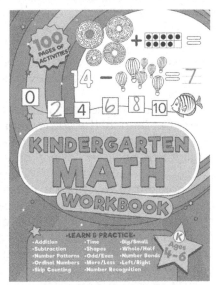

Made in United States
Orlando, FL
15 December 2024